EASY STRAWBERRY COOKBOOK

A STRAWBERRY COOKBOOK FOR STRAWBERRY LOVERS, FILLED WITH DELICIOUS STRAWBERRY RECIPES

By
BookSumo Press
Copyright © by Saxonberg Associates
All rights reserved

Published by
BookSumo Press, a DBA of Saxonberg Associates
http://www.booksumo.com/

About the Author.

BookSumo Press is a publisher of unique, easy, and healthy cookbooks.

Our cookbooks span all topics and all subjects. If you want a deep dive into the possibilities of cooking with any type of ingredient. Then BookSumo Press is your go to place for robust yet simple and delicious cookbooks and recipes. Whether you are looking for great tasting pressure cooker recipes or authentic ethic and cultural food. BookSumo Press has a delicious and easy cookbook for you.

With simple ingredients, and even simpler step-by-step instructions BookSumo cookbooks get everyone in the kitchen chefing delicious meals.

BookSumo is an independent publisher of books operating in the beautiful Garden State (NJ) and our team of chefs and kitchen experts are here to teach, eat, and be merry!

INTRODUCTION

Welcome to *The Effortless Chef Series*! Thank you for taking the time to purchase this cookbook.

Come take a journey into the delights of easy cooking. The point of this cookbook and all BookSumo Press cookbooks is to exemplify the effortless nature of cooking simply.

In this book we focus on Strawberry. You will find that even though the recipes are simple, the taste of the dishes are quite amazing.

So will you take an adventure in simple cooking? If the answer is yes please consult the table of contents to find the dishes you are most interested in.

Once you are ready, jump right in and start cooking.

— BookSumo Press

TABLE OF CONTENTS

About the Author. 2

Introduction 3

Table of Contents 4

Any Issues? Contact Us..8

Legal Notes...9

Common Abbreviations 10

Chapter 1: Easy Strawberry Recipes....................................11

   I ♥ Strawberry Drinks 11

   Strawberry Shortcake 101.. 13

   Bread for Brunch 15

   Weekend Breakfast Muffins... 18

   John the Juice Smoothie 21

   Grace's Strawberry Jam 23

   Northern California Lemonade..26

   5-Ingredient Crisp 28

   Perfect Strawberry Topping 30

Zanzibar Pie 32

Artisanal Syrup 35

Lunch Box Salad 37

Mediterranean Strawberries 40

Fruity Nachos 42

Fiesta Strawberry 45

Spring Sorbet 101 48

Strawberry Smoothie Bowl 51

alternative Jam 53

Mid-Summer Dessert 55

Pavlova 57

Kansas Lemonade 60

Lancaster Strawberries 62

Strawberry Party Platter 64

Fruity Cold Soup 66

Easy Torte 68

Saturday Night Pudding 71

How to Make Buckle 74

Countryside Cobbler 77

Lolly Strawberries 79

- Strawberry Cake with No-Bake 81
- Mountain Time Strawberries 83
- Potluck Mousse 85
- French Toast 101 88
- Hungarian Cookies 91
- Deliciously Moist Scones 94
- Traditional Punjabi Lassi 97
- Fruit Flavored Butter 99
- How to Make Glaze 101
- Tara's Tiramisu 103
- Kid's Favorite Strawberries 106
- Saturday Afternoon Drink 108
- Roman Strawberries 110
- Fruit Salsa 112
- Cute Strawberry Desserts 114
- Wednesday Breakfast Bread 116
- Strawberry Melody 119
- Strawberry & Orange Spring Rolls with Strawberry Sauce 121
- Strawberry & Banana Spring Rolls 124

Strawberry Pineapple Gazpacho 126

Chocolaty Strawberry Filled Crepes 128

A Strawberry Shortcake Sweet Doughnut 131

Jelly Doughnut II 133

THANKS FOR READING! JOIN THE CLUB AND KEEP ON COOKING WITH 6 MORE COOKBOOKS.... 136

Come On 138

Let's Be Friends :) 138

ANY ISSUES? CONTACT US

If you find that something important to you is missing from this book please contact us at info@booksumo.com.

We will take your concerns into consideration when the 2nd edition of this book is published. And we will keep you updated!

— BookSumo Press

LEGAL NOTES

ALL RIGHTS RESERVED. NO PART OF THIS BOOK MAY BE REPRODUCED OR TRANSMITTED IN ANY FORM OR BY ANY MEANS. PHOTOCOPYING, POSTING ONLINE, AND / OR DIGITAL COPYING IS STRICTLY PROHIBITED UNLESS WRITTEN PERMISSION IS GRANTED BY THE BOOK'S PUBLISHING COMPANY. LIMITED USE OF THE BOOK'S TEXT IS PERMITTED FOR USE IN REVIEWS WRITTEN FOR THE PUBLIC.

Common Abbreviations

cup(s)	C.
tablespoon	tbsp
teaspoon	tsp
ounce	oz.
pound	lb

*All units used are standard American measurements

Chapter 1: Easy Strawberry Recipes

I ♥ Strawberry Drinks

Ingredients

- 1 C. strawberry, sliced
- 1/2 C. milk
- 1/2 C. water
- 1/4 C. caster sugar
- 1/2-2/3 tsp vanilla

Directions

- Slice up enough fresh strawberries to fill one cup.
- In a food processor, add strawberries and remaining Ingredients and pulse till smooth.

Servings per Recipe: 2

Timing Information:

Preparation	5 mins
Total Time	5 mins

Nutritional Information:

Calories	161.8
Fat	2.4g
Cholesterol	8.5mg
Sodium	32.7mg
Carbohydrates	33.4g
Protein	2.4g

* Percent Daily Values are based on a 2,000 calorie diet.

Strawberry Shortcake 101

Ingredients

- 1 quart fresh strawberries
- 1/2 C. sugar
- 8 oz. cream cheese, softened
- 1 C. powdered sugar
- 1 (8 oz.) containers frozen whipped topping
- 1 (14 oz.) angel food cake, cut into cubes

Directions

- Wash, stem and halve the strawberries.
- In a bowl, add the strawberries and sugar and toss to coat well.
- Refrigerate to chill.
- In another bowl, add the cream cheese and powdered sugar and beat well.
- Fold in the whipped topping and cake cubes.
- Place the cake into an ungreased 13x9-inch baking dish.
- Refrigerate, covered for at least 2 hours.
- Cut the chilled cake into squares and serve with the topping of the strawberries.

Servings per Recipe: 12

Timing Information:

| Preparation | 20 mins |
| Total Time | 20 mins |

Nutritional Information:

Calories	296.8
Fat	11.5g
Cholesterol	20.8mg
Sodium	235.3mg
Carbohydrates	46.5g
Protein	3.7g

* Percent Daily Values are based on a 2,000 calorie diet.

Bread for Brunch

Ingredients

- 1 3/4 C. flour
- 1/2 tsp baking powder
- 1/4 tsp baking soda
- 1/2 tsp salt
- 1/4 tsp cinnamon
- 1/2 C. butter, softened
- 3/4 C. sugar
- 1/4 C. light brown sugar
- 2 eggs, room temperature
- 1/2 C. sour cream, room temperature
- 1 tsp vanilla
- 1 1/4 C. strawberries, fresh & coarsely chopped
- 3/4 C. walnuts (optional)

Directions

- Set your oven to 350 degrees F before doing anything else and grease an 8x4-inch loaf pan.
- In a large bowl, mix together the flour, baking powder, baking soda, salt and cinnamon and keep aside.
- In small bowl, add the butter and beat till creamy.

- Slowly, add the sugar, beating continuously till light and airy.
- Add the brown sugar and mix well.
- Add the eggs, one at a time, beating continuously till well combined.
- Add the sour cream and vanilla and beat till well combined.
- Add the flour mixture and mix till just moistened.
- Fold in the strawberries and walnuts.
- Transfer the mixture into the prepared loaf pan.
- Cook in the oven for about 60-65 minutes.
- Remove from the oven and keep onto wire rack for about 10 minutes.
- Carefully, invert the cakes onto wire rack to cool completely.

Servings per Recipe: 10

Timing Information:

Preparation	15 mins
Total Time	1 hr 15 mins

Nutritional Information:

Calories	283.7
Fat	12.7g
Cholesterol	67.5mg
Sodium	272.6mg
Carbohydrates	39.0g
Protein	3.9g

* Percent Daily Values are based on a 2,000 calorie diet.

Weekend Breakfast Muffins

Ingredients

- 2 C. flour
- 2 tbsp baking powder
- 1/2 tsp salt
- 1 C. sugar
- 6 tsp sugar
- 1 1/2 C. chopped strawberries
- 2 eggs
- 1/2-1 C. unsalted butter, melted
- 1/2 C. milk
- 1 tsp vanilla extract

Directions

- Set your oven to 375 degrees F before doing anything else and line the cups of muffin pans with the paper liners.
- In a large bowl, mix together the flour, baking powder, salt and 1 C. of the sugar.
- Add the strawberries and toss to coat well.
- In another bowl, add the eggs, butter, milk and vanilla and beat till well combined.
- Add the egg mixture Ingredients to the flour mixture and mix till just combined.

- Transfer the mixture into the prepared muffin cups evenly and sprinkle with 1/2 tsp of the sugar evenly.
- Cook in the oven for about 25 minutes or till a toothpick inserted in the center comes out clean.

Servings per Recipe: 1

Timing Information:

Preparation	10 mins
Total Time	35 mins

Nutritional Information:

Calories	242.6
Fat	9.0g
Cholesterol	52.7mg
Sodium	297.1mg
Carbohydrates	37.1g
Protein	3.7g

* Percent Daily Values are based on a 2,000 calorie diet.

JOHN THE JUICE SMOOTHIE

Ingredients

- 1 1/2 C. milk
- 1 C. strawberry
- 2 tbsp sugar
- 1 tsp lemon juice
- 1 C. crushed ice

Directions

- In a blender, add all the Ingredients and pulse till smooth.

Servings per Recipe: 1

Timing Information:

Preparation	5 mins
Total Time	5 mins

Nutritional Information:

Calories	168.4
Fat	6.1g
Cholesterol	22.7mg
Sodium	83.6mg
Carbohydrates	23.8g
Protein	5.7g

* Percent Daily Values are based on a 2,000 calorie diet.

Grace's Strawberry Jam

Ingredients

- 2 quarts strawberries, cut and crushed to yield 5 C. crushed berries
- 7 C. sugar
- 1/2 tsp butter
- 1 (1 3/4 oz.) boxes pectin

Directions

- In a bowl, place the sugar and keep aside.
- In a large boiler, place the crushed berries.
- Add the package of Sure-Jell and mix.
- Add the butter and bring to a boil.
- Add the sugar and cook, stirring continuously.
- Again bring to a boil and boil for about 1 minute, stirring continuously.
- Remove from the heat and with a metal spoon, skim foam from the top.
- Immediately, transfer the mixture into the cleaned and preheated jars.
- With clean hot cloth, clean the rims of the jars.
- Place the heated lids on jars and tighten the rings.
- Arrange the jars in water bath canner for about 5 minutes.

- Remove the jars from canner and turn them upside down for about 5 minutes.
- Return the jars to upright position and keep in room temperature to cool completely before storing.

Servings per Recipe: 1

Timing Information:

Preparation	30 mins
Total Time	45 mins

Nutritional Information:

Calories	997.7
Fat	0.9g
Cholesterol	0.8mg
Sodium	23.8mg
Carbohydrates	256.3g
Protein	1.3g

* Percent Daily Values are based on a 2,000 calorie diet.

Northern California Lemonade

Ingredients

- 3 C. water, cold
- 1 quart fresh strawberries
- 3/4 C. sugar
- 3/4 C. lemon juice
- 2 C. club soda, cold
- Lemon slice (optional)

Directions

- In a blender, add the water, strawberries and sugar and pulse till smooth.
- Add the lemon juice and soda and pulse till combined.
- Serve immediately with a garnishing of the lemon slices.

Servings per Recipe: 8

Timing Information:

Preparation	10 mins
Total Time	10 mins

Nutritional Information:

Calories	100.6
Fat	0.2g
Cholesterol	0.0mg
Sodium	16.2mg
Carbohydrates	25.8g
Protein	0.5g

* Percent Daily Values are based on a 2,000 calorie diet.

5-Ingredient Crisp

Ingredients

- 1 tbsp butter
- 1/2 C. uncooked oatmeal
- 1/4 C. packed brown sugar
- 1/2 tsp cinnamon
- 1 C. sliced strawberry

Directions

- Set your oven to 375 degrees F before doing anything else.
- In a small pan, melt the butter on low heat.
- Add the oatmeal, brown sugar and cinnamon and mix well.
- Immediately, remove from the heat.
- Place the strawberries in 2 oven-proof dishes evenly and top with the oatmeal mixture.
- Cook in the oven for about 15 minutes.

Servings per Recipe: 2

Timing Information:

Preparation	10 mins
Total Time	25 mins

Nutritional Information:

Calories	256.8
Fat	7.3g
Cholesterol	15.2mg
Sodium	60.3mg
Carbohydrates	46.7g
Protein	3.2g

* Percent Daily Values are based on a 2,000 calorie diet.

Perfect Strawberry Topping

Ingredients

- 2 lb. ripe strawberries, hulled
- 1/2 C. granulated sugar
- 2 tsp cornstarch
- 1/2 lemon, juice of
- 1 pinch salt

Directions

- In a medium pan, mix together all the Ingredients on medium-low heat and cook for about 10 minutes, stirring gently.
- Remove from heat and keep aside to cool.

Servings per Recipe: 12

Timing Information:

Preparation	10 mins
Total Time	20 mins

Nutritional Information:

Calories	58.6
Fat	0.2g
Cholesterol	0.0mg
Sodium	13.8mg
Carbohydrates	14.7g
Protein	0.5g

* Percent Daily Values are based on a 2,000 calorie diet.

Zanzibar Pie

Ingredients

- 3 eggs, beaten
- 2 1/2 C. rhubarb, red, 1 inch slices
- 1 1/4 C. sugar
- 1 1/2 C. strawberries, fresh, sliced
- 1/4 C. enriched flour
- 1 9" pastry crust with lattice top
- 1/4 tsp salt
- 1 tbsp butter
- 1/2 tsp nutmeg
- Whole strawberries, as required

Directions

- Set your oven to 400 degrees F before doing anything else.
- In a large bowl, add the eggs, sugar, flour, salt and nutmeg and mix well.
- In another bowl, mix together the rhubarb and sliced strawberries.
- Arrange the pastry crust into a 9-inch pie dish.
- Place the strawberry mixture over the crust evenly and top with the egg mixture evenly.

- Place the butter on top in the form of dots.
- Arrange the lattice crust on top, crimping the edge high.
- Cook in the oven for about 40 minutes.
- Fill the openings of the lattice crust with whole strawberries.
- Serve warm.

Servings per Recipe: 6

Timing Information:

| Preparation | 0 mins |
| Total Time | 40 mins |

Nutritional Information:

Calories	343.4
Fat	10.3g
Cholesterol	98.0mg
Sodium	308.6mg
Carbohydrates	58.7g
Protein	5.4g

* Percent Daily Values are based on a 2,000 calorie diet.

Artisanal Syrup

Ingredients

- 1 pint fresh strawberries
- 2 C. sugar
- 1/4 tsp lemon juice

Directions

- In a food processor, add the strawberries and pulse till smooth.
- Through a wire-mesh strainer, strain the strawberry puree into a pan
- Discard the seeds.
- In the pan, add the sugar and juice on low heat and cook till the sugar dissolves, stirring continuously.
- Increase the heat to medium-high and bring to a boil.
- Reduce the heat and simmer for about 5 minutes, skimming the froth from the top.
- Remove from the heat and keep aside to cool.

Servings per Recipe: 1

Timing Information:

Preparation	10 mins
Total Time	15 mins

Nutritional Information:

Calories	738.9
Fat	0.4g
Cholesterol	0.0mg
Sodium	3.3mg
Carbohydrates	189.9g
Protein	1.0g

* Percent Daily Values are based on a 2,000 calorie diet.

Lunch Box Salad

Ingredients

- 2 C. crushed pretzels
- 3/4 C. butter, melted
- 3 tbsp white sugar
- 1 (8 oz.) packages cream cheese, softened
- 1 C. white sugar
- 1 (8 oz.) cartons frozen whipped topping, thawed
- 2 (3 oz.) packages strawberry gelatin
- 2 C. boiling water
- 2 (10 oz.) packages frozen strawberries

Directions

- Set your oven to 400 degrees F before doing anything else.
- In a bowl, add the crushed pretzels, melted butter and 3 tbsp of the white sugar and mix till well combined.
- In the bottom of 13x9-inch baking dish, place the pretzel mixture and press to smooth the surface.
- Cook in the oven for about 8-10 minutes.
- Remove from the oven and keep aside to cool.
- In a large bowl, add the cream cheese and white sugar and beat till creamy.

- Fold in the whipped topping.
- Place the cream cheese mixture over the cooled crust.
- In a bowl of the boiling water, dissolve the gelatin.
- Stir in the frozen strawberries and keep aside to set slightly.
- Place the strawberry mixture over the cream cheese mixture evenly.
- Refrigerate till set completely.

Servings per Recipe: 18

Timing Information:

Preparation	35 mins
Total Time	45 mins

Nutritional Information:

Calories	345.4
Fat	15.9g
Cholesterol	34.2mg
Sodium	499.3mg
Carbohydrates	48.2g
Protein	4.4g

* Percent Daily Values are based on a 2,000 calorie diet.

Mediterranean Strawberries

Ingredients

- 1 pint ripe strawberry
- 2 tbsp sugar
- 2 tbsp balsamic vinegar

Directions

- Hull the strawberries and cut into quarters lengthwise.
- In a bowl, add the strawberries, vinegar and sugar and toss to coat well.
- Cover the bowl and keep aside for about 1 hour.
- Now, refrigerate to chill for about 1 hour.
- Remove from the refrigerator and toss again before serving.

Servings per Recipe: 6

Timing Information:

| Preparation | 15 mins |
| Total Time | 2 hrs 15 mins |

Nutritional Information:

Calories	39.9
Fat	0.1g
Cholesterol	0.0mg
Sodium	1.8mg
Carbohydrates	9.6g
Protein	0.4g

* Percent Daily Values are based on a 2,000 calorie diet.

FRUITY NACHOS

Ingredients

- 3 C. sliced fresh strawberries
- 1/4 C. sugar
- 1/4 C. almond flavored liqueur (such as Amaretto)
- 3/4 C. sour cream
- 2 tbsp sugar
- 1/4 tsp cinnamon
- 6 6-inch flour tortillas
- 2 tbsp melted butter
- 2 tsp sugar
- 1/4 tsp cinnamon
- 2 tbsp sliced almonds, toasted
- 1 tbsp shaved semisweet chocolate

Directions

- In a bowl, add the strawberries, 1/4 C. of the sugar and almond-flavored liqueur and mix well.
- Refrigerate, covered for at least 1 hour.
- In another bowl, add the sour cream, 2 tbsp of the sugar and 1/4 tsp of the cinnamon and mix till well combined.
- Refrigerate, covered till using.

- Set your oven to 400 degrees F.
- With a pastry brush, lightly coat 1 side of the tortillas with the melted butter.
- Cut each tortilla into 6 equal sized wedges.
- Place the tortilla wedges onto 2 ungreased baking sheets in a single layer and sprinkle with 2 tsp of the sugar and 1/4 tsp of the cinnamon.
- Cook in the oven for about 6-8 minutes.
- Remove from the oven and keep aside to cool.
- Remove the strawberries from the refrigerator and drain completely.
- Divide the tortilla wedges into 6 dessert bowls and top with the strawberries and a little of the sour cream mixture.
- Serve with a topping of the toasted almonds and shaved chocolate.

Servings per Recipe: 6

Timing Information:

Preparation	1 hr 30 mins
Total Time	1 hr 38 mins

Nutritional Information:

Calories	284.3
Fat	14.0g
Cholesterol	22.8mg
Sodium	234.4mg
Carbohydrates	37.0g
Protein	4.5g

* Percent Daily Values are based on a 2,000 calorie diet.

Fiesta Strawberry

Ingredients

- 1 angel food cake
- 1 (16 oz.) containers Cool Whip
- 8 oz. cream cheese
- 1 C. sugar, divided
- 1 tsp vanilla extract
- 1 quart fresh strawberries, sliced
- 3 tbsp cornstarch
- 1 (3 oz.) packages strawberry Jell-O gelatin dessert
- 1 tbsp lemon juice
- 1 C. water

Directions

- In a medium pan, add 1/2 C. of the sugar, cornstarch, Jell-O, lemon juice and water on medium heat and cook till mixture becomes thick, stirring continuously.
- Remove from the heat and keep aside to cool slightly.
- Add the sliced strawberries and stir to combine.
- Torn the angel food cake into 1-inch pieces.
- In a bowl, add the cake pieces and 2 C. of the Cool Whip and toss to coat.

- In another bowl, add the cream cheese, 1/2 C. of the remaining sugar and vanilla and beat till smooth.
- Stir in the remaining Cool Whip.
- In a 13x9-inch baking dish, place the cake mixture and press to smooth the surface.
- Place the cream cheese mixture over the cake mixture evenly and top with the cooled strawberry mixture.
- Refrigerate for about 2-3 hours before serving.

Servings per Recipe: 15

Timing Information:

| Preparation | 45 mins |
| Total Time | 45 mins |

Nutritional Information:

Calories	343.6
Fat	13.1g
Cholesterol	16.6mg
Sodium	281.8mg
Carbohydrates	53.6g
Protein	4.6g

* Percent Daily Values are based on a 2,000 calorie diet.

Spring Sorbet 101

Ingredients

- 1 C. water
- 3/4 C. sugar
- 1 pint fresh strawberries
- 1/2 C. orange juice

Directions

- Combine water & sugar in a pan, stir over low heat until sugar dissolves.
- Bring to a boil & boil gently for 5 minutes without stirring.
- Set aside to cool.
- Wash berries.
- Remove caps.
- Puree fruit in a blender or food processor until almost smooth.
- In a medium bowl, combine fruit with cooled syrup and orange juice.
- If you have an ice cream freezer, you can put the puree mixture into that & process using the directions
- In a pan, add the water and sugar on low heat and cook till the sugar dissolves, stirring continuously.

- Bring to a boil and then boil for about 5 minutes without stirring.
- Remove from the heat and keep aside to cool.
- Wash the strawberries and hull them.
- In a blender, add the strawberries and pulse till smooth.
- In a bowl, mix together the strawberry puree, cooled sugar syrup and orange juice.
- Transfer the mixture into ice cream maker and process according to manufacturers

Servings per Recipe: 6

Timing Information:

| Preparation | 20 mins |
| Total Time | 2 hrs 20 mins |

Nutritional Information:

Calories	125.0
Fat	0.2g
Cholesterol	0.0mg
Sodium	1.5mg
Carbohydrates	31.7g
Protein	0.5g

* Percent Daily Values are based on a 2,000 calorie diet.

Strawberry Smoothie Bowl

Ingredients

- 500 g strawberries, hulled
- 2 large egg whites, at room temperature
- 1/2 C. caster sugar
- 1/2 C. whipping cream
- 1/4-1/2 tsp vanilla
- 6 -8 strawberries, sliced, for garnish
- Mint leaf

Directions

- In a blender, add the strawberries and pulse till smooth.
- In a bowl, add the strawberry puree, egg whites and sugar and beat till stiff and glossy.
- In another bowl, add the cream and vanilla and beat till peaks form.
- Gently fold the cream mixture into the strawberry mixture.
- Transfer the mixture into a serving bowl and top with the strawberry slices and mint.
- With a plastic wrap, cover the bowl and refrigerate before serving.

Servings per Recipe: 8

Timing Information:

Preparation	15 mins
Total Time	15 mins

Nutritional Information:

Calories	127.2
Fat	5.7g
Cholesterol	20.3mg
Sodium	20.2mg
Carbohydrates	18.4g
Protein	1.6g

* Percent Daily Values are based on a 2,000 calorie diet.

ALTERNATIVE JAM

Ingredients

- 2 1/2 C. coarsely chopped hulled strawberries
- 1/2 C. sugar
- 2 1/2 tbsp cornstarch

Directions

- In a heavy small pan, add all the Ingredients and bring to a boil, crushing the berries slightly with the back of spoon.
- Now, boil for about 2 minutes, stirring continuously.
- Transfer the mixture into a bowl and refrigerate to cool completely.

Servings per Recipe: 1

Timing Information:

Preparation	0 mins
Total Time	5 mins

Nutritional Information:

Calories	578.4
Fat	1.0g
Cholesterol	0.0mg
Sodium	6.4mg
Carbohydrates	145.8g
Protein	2.4g

* Percent Daily Values are based on a 2,000 calorie diet.

Mid-Summer Dessert

Ingredients

- 1 angel food cake
- 1 (1 lb) container frozen strawberries, with juice, thawed
- 1 (6 oz.) packages strawberry Jell-O gelatin dessert
- 1 1/4 C. boiling water
- 1 pint heavy cream, whipped

Directions

- Tear the angel cake into small pieces and transfer into a bowl.
- In 1 1/4 C. of the boiling water, dissolve the Jell-O.
- Add the strawberries and juices and stir to combine.
- Keep aside to cool completely.
- After cooling, fold in the whipped cream.
- Place the strawberry mixture over the angel cake pieces and stir to combine.
- Transfer the mixture into a bundt pan and refrigerate till firm.
- Carefully, invert the cake onto a serving platter and cut into desired slices.
- Serve with a topping of the whipped cream and strawberries.

Servings per Recipe: 1

Timing Information:

| Preparation | 30 mins |
| Total Time | 30 mins |

Nutritional Information:

Calories	3980.5
Fat	178.4g
Cholesterol	652.1mg
Sodium	4036.6mg
Carbohydrates	558.4g
Protein	61.3g

* Percent Daily Values are based on a 2,000 calorie diet.

Pavlova

Ingredients

- 3 egg whites
- 1 pinch cream of tartar
- 3/4 C. granulated sugar
- 1 tsp vanilla
- 2 C. whipping cream
- 4 C. strawberries, sliced

Directions

- Set your oven to 275 degrees F before doing anything else and line a baking sheet with a piece of foil.
- In a large bowl, add the egg whites and cream of tartar and beat till soft peaks form.
- Add the sugar, 1 tbsp at a time and beat till glossy peaks form.
- Add the vanilla and beat till well combined.
- Place the meringue onto the prepared baking sheet into a 10-inch circle, pushing up the edges to form a slight ridge.
- Cook in the oven for about 1 1/2 hours.
- Turn off the oven but leave the meringue in the oven to dry completely.
- Remove from the oven.

- Carefully, remove the foil and keep aside to cool completely.
- Arrange the meringue onto a serving platter.
- Spread the whipped cream over the meringue and top with the strawberries.
- Cut into the wedges and serve.

Servings per Recipe: 8

Timing Information:

Preparation	30 mins
Total Time	2 hrs

Nutritional Information:

Calories	308.8
Fat	22.2g
Cholesterol	81.5mg
Sodium	44.1mg
Carbohydrates	26.1g
Protein	3.0g

* Percent Daily Values are based on a 2,000 calorie diet.

Kansas Lemonade

Ingredients

- 1 C. lemon juice
- 1 C. sugar
- 1 1/2 C. strawberries, washed and hulled
- 2 tbsp light corn syrup
- Water, to fill 2 quart pitcher

Directions

- In a blender, add the strawberries and corn syrup and pulse till smooth.
- Through a fine sieve, strain the strawberry puree and discard the pulp and seeds.
- In a 2 quart pitcher, add the strawberry puree, lemon juice and sugar and mix till the sugar is dissolved.
- In serving glasses, place the ice.
- Pour the lemonade over the ice and serve.

Servings per Recipe: 6

Timing Information:

Preparation	30 mins
Total Time	30 mins

Nutritional Information:

Calories	171.4
Fat	0.1g
Cholesterol	0.0mg
Sodium	5.3mg
Carbohydrates	45.2g
Protein	0.4g

* Percent Daily Values are based on a 2,000 calorie diet.

LANCASTER STRAWBERRIES

Ingredients

- 8 oz. cream cheese
- 1 C. whipping cream
- 1/2 tsp vanilla extract
- Strawberry, 1 C. for each serving
- Powdered sugar
- Mint leaves

Directions

- In a bowl, add the cream cheese and beat till softened.
- Slowly, add the cream and beat till the mixture is smooth.
- Stir in the vanilla extract and powdered sugar.
- Wash and hull the strawberries and transfer into another bowl.
- Refrigerate the bowls of strawberries and cream mixture till serving.
- Divide the strawberries into serving dishes bowls and top with the cream mixture.
- Serve with a garnishing of the garnish mint leaves.

Servings per Recipe: 4

Timing Information:

| Preparation | 5 mins |
| Total Time | 5 mins |

Nutritional Information:

Calories	401.0
Fat	41.4g
Cholesterol	144.0mg
Sodium	204.9mg
Carbohydrates	4.0g
Protein	4.5g

* Percent Daily Values are based on a 2,000 calorie diet.

Strawberry Party Platter

Ingredients

- 16 oz. sharp cheddar cheese, grated
- 1 (3 oz.) packages cream cheese, softened
- 3/4 C. mayonnaise
- 1 small onion, chopped
- 1 C. chopped pecans
- 1/2 tsp garlic powder
- Cayenne pepper
- 1 C. strawberry preserves

Directions

- In a food processor, add all the Ingredients and pulse till well combined.
- Transfer into a bowl and refrigerate for about 2-3 hours.
- Now, transfer the mixture onto a platter.
- With your hands, mold the mixture into a ring formation and top with the strawberry preserves evenly.
- Serve alongside the buttery crackers.

Servings per Recipe: 20

Timing Information:

| Preparation | 10 mins |
| Total Time | 3 hrs 10 mins |

Nutritional Information:

Calories	189.9
Fat	12.9g
Cholesterol	28.5mg
Sodium	160.0mg
Carbohydrates	12.6g
Protein	6.5g

* Percent Daily Values are based on a 2,000 calorie diet.

Fruity Cold Soup

Ingredients

- 1 C. strawberry, chopped
- 1 C. cold milk
- 2 -3 tbsp sugar

Directions

- In a serving bowl, add the strawberries and sprinkle with the sugar.
- Keep aside for about 10-15 minutes.
- Now, place the milk and mix well.
- Serve immediately.

Servings per Recipe: 1

Timing Information:

| Preparation | 25 mins |
| Total Time | 25 mins |

Nutritional Information:

Calories	299.7
Fat	9.3g
Cholesterol	34.1mg
Sodium	121.2mg
Carbohydrates	47.6g
Protein	8.9g

* Percent Daily Values are based on a 2,000 calorie diet.

Easy Torte

Ingredients

CRUST

- 1/2 C. pecans, toasted
- 1 1/2 C. flour
- 2 tbsp sugar
- 3/4 C. cold butter

FILLING

- 8 oz. cream cheese, room temperature
- 1/2 C. sugar
- 1 C. whipping cream
- 3 C. fresh strawberries, halved

Directions

- Set your oven to 325 degrees F before doing anything else.
- In a food processor, add the pecans and pulse till finely chopped.
- Add the flour and sugar and pulse till well combined.
- Add the cold butter, 2 tbsp at a time and pulse till well combined.

- Place the mixture into a spring form pan, pressing the mixture 1-inch up the sides of the pan.
- Cook in the oven for about 30-40 minutes.
- Remove from the oven and keep aside to cool.
- In a bowl, add the cream cheese and sugar and with an electric mixer, beat on high speed till fluffy.
- While the motor is still running slowly, add the whipping cream in a steady small stream, beating till well combined.
- Place the cream cheese mixture over the cooled crust evenly.
- Refrigerate, covered for up to 24 hours.
- Carefully, remove the torte from the spring form pan and top with the halved strawberries.
- Cut into desired wedges and serve.

Servings per Recipe: 12

Timing Information:

Preparation	20 mins
Total Time	50 mins

Nutritional Information:

Calories	375.0
Fat	28.8g
Cholesterol	78.5mg
Sodium	170.3mg
Carbohydrates	27.0g
Protein	3.9g

* Percent Daily Values are based on a 2,000 calorie diet.

SATURDAY NIGHT PUDDING

Ingredients

- 2 lb. small strawberries
- 1 C. sugar
- 1 quart water
- 1/3 C. cornstarch
- 1/2 tsp vanilla (optional)
- 1/2 tsp finely grated lemon zest (optional)

Directions

- Clean and rinse the strawberries.
- In a pan, add the water and bring to a boil on medium heat.
- Add the sugar and strawberries and simmer for about 8 minutes, breaking the berries with the back of a spoon.
- Meanwhile in a bowl, add a little water and dissolve the cornstarch.
- Slowly, add the cornstarch mixture in the pan, stirring continuously.
- Add the vanilla and lemon zest and bring to a boil, stirring continuously.
- Boil for a few minutes, stirring continuously.

- Transfer the mixture into a bowl and refrigerator to cool completely.
- Serve with a topping of your liking.

Servings per Recipe: 8

Timing Information:

Preparation	15 mins
Total Time	35 mins

Nutritional Information:

Calories	153.4
Fat	0.3g
Cholesterol	0.0mg
Sodium	5.4mg
Carbohydrates	38.5g
Protein	0.7g

* Percent Daily Values are based on a 2,000 calorie diet.

How to Make Buckle

Ingredients

- 1/4 C. butter, softened
- 3/4 C. sugar
- 1 egg, beaten
- 1/2 tsp vanilla
- 1/2 C. milk
- 2 C. flour, sifted
- 2 tsp baking powder
- 1/2 tsp salt
- 2 C. fresh strawberries, sliced

TOPPING

- 1/4 C. butter, softened
- 1/2 C. brown sugar
- 1/3 C. flour, sifted
- 1/2 tsp cinnamon
- 1 dash nutmeg

Directions

- Set your oven to 375 degrees F before doing anything else and lightly, grease a 9x9-inch baking dish.

- In a large bowl, add the sugar and butter and beat till light and fluffy.
- Add the eggs and vanilla and beat till well combined.
- Add the milk and beat till well combined.
- In another bowl, sift together the flour, baking powder and salt.
- Add the egg mixture into the flour mixture and mix till well combined.
- Fold in the strawberries.
- Transfer the mixture into the prepared baking dish evenly.
- For topping in a bowl, add the butter and sugar and beat till creamy.
- Add the flour and cinnamon and mix well.
- Spread the flour mixture over the strawberry mixture evenly and sprinkle with the nutmeg.
- Cook in the oven for about 30-35 minutes.
- Serve warm with the topping of the cream.

Servings per Recipe: 10

Timing Information:

Preparation	10 mins
Total Time	10 mins

Nutritional Information:

Calories	312.8
Fat	10.5g
Cholesterol	47.2mg
Sodium	272.4mg
Carbohydrates	51.1g
Protein	4.3g

* Percent Daily Values are based on a 2,000 calorie diet.

Countryside Cobbler

Ingredients

- 4 C. strawberries, cleaned and sliced
- 1 C. all-purpose flour
- 1/2 tsp baking powder
- 1 C. sugar
- 1 egg, beaten
- 1/4 C. butter, in cubes

Directions

- Set your oven to 375 degrees F before doing anything else.
- In a bowl, mix together the flour, baking powder and sugar.
- Add the egg and with a fork, mix till a crumbly mixture forms.
- In the bottom of a 9-inch square baking dish, place the strawberries and top with the flour mixture evenly.
- Place the butter on top in the form of the dots.
- Cook in the oven for about 45-50 minutes.
- Remove from the oven and keep on wire rack to cool slightly.
- Serve warm.

Servings per Recipe: 4

Timing Information:

Preparation	10 mins
Total Time	1 hr

Nutritional Information:

Calories	473.2
Fat	13.4g
Cholesterol	77.0mg
Sodium	167.0mg
Carbohydrates	85.1g
Protein	5.8g

* Percent Daily Values are based on a 2,000 calorie diet.

LOLLY STRAWBERRIES

Ingredients

- 4 C. fresh strawberries
- 4 tbsp sour cream
- 4 tsp brown sugar

Directions

- Wash, hull and drain the strawberries completely.
- Divide the strawberries in 4 dessert bowls and top with the sour cream evenly.
- Serve with a sprinkling of the brown sugar.

Servings per Recipe: 4

Timing Information:

Preparation	5 mins
Total Time	5 mins

Nutritional Information:

Calories	89.1
Fat	2.9g
Cholesterol	5.2mg
Sodium	9.5mg
Carbohydrates	16.0g
Protein	1.3g

* Percent Daily Values are based on a 2,000 calorie diet.

Strawberry Cake with No-Bake

Ingredients

- 4 C. strawberries, frozen, halved
- 1/2 C. coconut cream
- 2 C. pineapple juice, chilled
- 1/2 C. crushed pineapple
- 2 tsp whipped cream
- 2 large strawberries
- 1 tsp white sugar

Directions

- In a food processor, add the strawberries, coconut cream, pineapple juice and crushed pineapple and pulse till smooth.
- Divide the strawberry mixture into 2 chilled glasses.
- Place the dollop of the whipped cream in the center of each glass and arrange 1 strawberry beside the whipped cream.
- Serve with a sprinkling of the sugar.

Servings per Recipe: 2

Timing Information:

Preparation	5 mins
Total Time	10 mins

Nutritional Information:

Calories	420.5
Fat	14.6g
Cholesterol	0.7mg
Sodium	46.9mg
Carbohydrates	73.8g
Protein	5.2g

* Percent Daily Values are based on a 2,000 calorie diet.

Mountain Time Strawberries

Ingredients

- 8 large strawberries, whole & cleaned
- 1 tbsp balsamic vinegar
- 1 tbsp sugar

Directions

- Set your grill for high heat and lightly, grease the grill grate.
- Dip the strawberries in the balsamic vinegar evenly and then coat with the sugar.
- Cook the strawberries on the grill for about 1-2 minutes.
- Remove from the grill and serve immediately.

Servings per Recipe: 4

Timing Information:

Preparation	2 mins
Total Time	4 mins

Nutritional Information:

Calories	27.2
Fat	0.1g
Cholesterol	0.0mg
Sodium	1.3mg
Carbohydrates	6.6g
Protein	0.2g

* Percent Daily Values are based on a 2,000 calorie diet.

Potluck Mousse

Ingredients

- 1 lb ripe strawberry, hulled and sliced
- 2 tbsp granulated sugar
- 1 tbsp kirsch
- 1/2 C. confectioners' sugar
- 1 1/4 C. heavy cream

Directions

- In a bowl, add half of the strawberries and sprinkle with the granulated sugar and kirsch.
- Keep aside for about 15 minutes.
- In a blender, add the remaining strawberries and confectioners' sugar and pulse till smooth.
- In another bowl, add the cream and beat till stiff peaks form.
- In a small bowl, add 1/4 of the whipped cream reserve for the garnishing in refrigerator.
- Gently, fold the remaining cream into the strawberries puree.
- Divide the strawberry mixture in 4 balloon-shaped wine glasses, reserving a few strawberry slices for garnish.
- Fill each glass with the strawberry cream evenly.

- With the plastic wraps, cover the glasses and refrigerate for a few hours.
- Place the reserved whipped cream in a pastry bag, fitted with a star tip and decorate the mousse.
- Serve with a garnishing of the remaining strawberries slices.

Servings per Recipe: 4

Timing Information:

Preparation	30 mins
Total Time	30 mins

Nutritional Information:

Calories	375.7
Fat	27.8g
Cholesterol	101.8mg
Sodium	29.7mg
Carbohydrates	32.0g
Protein	2.2g

* Percent Daily Values are based on a 2,000 calorie diet.

French Toast 101

Ingredients

- 1 (3 oz.) packages cream cheese, softened
- 2 tbsp confectioners' sugar
- 2 tbsp strawberry preserves
- 8 slices country white bread
- 2 eggs
- 1/2 C. half-and-half
- 2 tbsp granulated sugar
- 4 tbsp butter

Directions

- In a small bowl, add the cream cheese and confectioners' sugar and mix well.
- Add the strawberry preserves and mix well.
- Place the cream cheese mixture over 4 bread slices evenly and cover with the remaining bread slices to form the sandwiches.
- In a shallow bowl, add the eggs, half-and-half and granulated sugar and beat till well combined.
- Dip each sandwich in the egg mixture evenly.
- In a large skillet, melt 2 tbsp of the butter on medium heat and cook 2 sandwiches for about 1-2 minutes per side.

- Repeat with the remaining butter and sandwiches.
- Slice the sandwiches in half diagonally and serve immediately.

Servings per Recipe: 4

Timing Information:

Preparation	10 mins
Total Time	20 mins

Nutritional Information:

Calories	449.9
Fat	26.3g
Cholesterol	158.1mg
Sodium	476.4mg
Carbohydrates	44.7g
Protein	9.2g

* Percent Daily Values are based on a 2,000 calorie diet.

Hungarian Cookies

Ingredients

- 3 C. unbleached all-purpose flour
- 1 C. butter, softened
- 1/4 C. sugar
- 1/2 tsp salt
- 1 (1/4 oz.) package active dry yeast
- 1/2 C. warm milk
- 1 large egg
- 1 tsp vanilla extract
- 1/2 C. strawberry preserves
- 1 large egg, well beaten

GLAZE

- 2/3 C. confectioners' sugar
- 1 tsp almond extract
- 2 1/2 tsp milk

Directions

- In a large bowl, add the flour, butter, sugar and salt and with your hand mixer, beat till a coarse crumb like mixture forms.
- In a small bowl, add 1/2 C. of the warm milk and dissolve the yeast completely.

- Add 1 egg and vanilla and stir to combine.
- Add the milk mixture into flour the mixture, and with the electric mixer, beat on low speed till well combined.
- Divide the dough 2 equal sized portions.
- With wax papers, cover the both dough portions and refrigerate for about 1 hour.
- Set your oven to 350 degrees F and line a large cookie sheet with the parchment paper.
- Remove the dough portions from the refrigerator and place onto a lightly floured surface.
- Roll the both portions into 1/8-1/4-inch thickness.
- Cut each dough portion into 3-inch squares.
- Place about 1 tsp of the strawberry preserves over each square.
- Bring up 2 opposite corners of each square to center and then pinch tightly to seal the filling.
- Arrange the cookies onto the prepared cookie sheet about 2-inch apart.
- Coat all cookies with the beaten egg slightly.
- Cook in the oven for about 10-14 minutes.
- Remove from the oven and keep on the wire rack for about 10 minutes.
- Carefully, invert the cookies onto wire rack to cool completely.
- For glaze in a bowl, add the powdered sugar, almond extract and milk and mix till well combined.
- Serve the cookies with a drizzling of the glaze.

Servings per Recipe: 12

Timing Information:

| Preparation | 15 mins |
| Total Time | 29 mins |

Nutritional Information:

Calories	351.7
Fat	16.9g
Cholesterol	77.4mg
Sodium	228.3mg
Carbohydrates	44.7g
Protein	5.0g

* Percent Daily Values are based on a 2,000 calorie diet.

DELICIOUSLY MOIST SCONES

Ingredients

- 2 C. all-purpose flour
- 1/4 C. packed brown sugar
- 2 tsp baking powder
- 1/4 tsp salt
- 2 tsp grated orange rind
- 4 tbsp chilled butter, cut into small pieces
- 1 C. diced fresh strawberries
- 2/3 C. milk

Directions

- Set your oven to 425 degrees F before doing anything else.
- In a large bowl, add the flour, brown sugar, baking powder, salt and orange peel and mix till well combined.
- With a pastry blender, cut in the butter till a crumbly mixture forms.
- Fold in the strawberries.
- Slowly, add enough milk and mix till a soft dough forms.
- Make a ball from the dough.
- Place the dough ball onto a lightly floured surface and knead till a sticky dough forms.

- With your hands, pat the dough into a (3/4-inch thick) 7-inch round.
- Cut the dough into 8 equal sized wedges.
- Arrange the dough wedges onto an ungreased baking sheet in a single layer about 1/2-inch apart.
- Cook in the oven for about 20-25 minutes.

Servings per Recipe: 8

Timing Information:

Preparation	20 mins
Total Time	45 mins

Nutritional Information:

Calories	210.6
Fat	6.8g
Cholesterol	18.1mg
Sodium	226.8mg
Carbohydrates	33.3g
Protein	4.0g

* Percent Daily Values are based on a 2,000 calorie diet.

TRADITIONAL PUNJABI LASSI

Ingredients

- 1 lb strawberry, chopped
- 1 C. Greek yogurt
- 1/3 C. honey
- 1/2 tsp salt
- 1/2 tsp cardamom powder
- 1 C. ice, crushed

Directions

- In a blender, add all the Ingredients and pulse till frothy.
- Transfer into 2 serving glasses and serve immediately.

Servings per Recipe: 2

Timing Information:

Preparation	10 mins
Total Time	10 mins

Nutritional Information:

Calories	245.9
Fat	0.7g
Cholesterol	0.0mg
Sodium	586.4mg
Carbohydrates	64.3g
Protein	1.7g

* Percent Daily Values are based on a 2,000 calorie diet.

Fruit Flavored Butter

Ingredients

- 1/2 C. unsalted butter, room temperature
- 1/4 C. strawberry preserves
- 1/8 C. fresh strawberries, chopped

Directions

- In a bowl, add the butter and beat till creamy.
- Add the strawberry preserves, 1 tbsp at a time and beat till well combined.
- Fold in the fresh strawberries.
- Refrigerate till serving.
- Remove from the refrigerator and keep in the room temperature to soften without stirring.

Servings per Recipe: 20

Timing Information:

Preparation	5 mins
Total Time	5 mins

Nutritional Information:

Calories	52.1
Fat	4.6g
Cholesterol	12.2mg
Sodium	1.9mg
Carbohydrates	2.8g
Protein	0.0g

* Percent Daily Values are based on a 2,000 calorie diet.

How to Make Glaze

Ingredients

- 1 C. strawberry, washed and hulled
- 1/2 C. sugar
- 1 1/2 tbsp cornstarch
- 2 tbsp Grand Marnier

Directions

- In a bowl, add the strawberries and with a potato masher, mash them.
- In a heavy pan, add the mashed strawberries, sugar and cornstarch on medium heat and cook till mixture becomes thick, stirring continuously.
- Stir in the Grand Marnier and immediately, remove from the heat.
- Transfer the mixture into a bowl, and refrigerate, covered to chill completely.

Servings per Recipe: 1

Timing Information:

| Preparation | 5 mins |
| Total Time | 10 mins |

Nutritional Information:

Calories	638.4
Fat	0.5g
Cholesterol	0.0mg
Sodium	4.6mg
Carbohydrates	162.6g
Protein	1.3g

* Percent Daily Values are based on a 2,000 calorie diet.

Tara's Tiramisu

Ingredients

- 2 eggs, at room temperature, separated
- 1/4 C. caster sugar
- 300 g mascarpone
- 1/2 C. whipped cream
- 15 strawberries, hulled and quartered
- 1/3 C. strong coffee
- 2 tbsp rum, optional
- 14 ladyfingers
- Cocoa, to dust
- 1 strawberry

Directions

- In a large bowl, add the egg yolks and sugar and with an electric mixer, beat till pale and thick.
- Add the mascarpone and beat well.
- In a small bowl, add the egg whites and beat till soft peaks form.
- Fold the whipped cream into the mascarpone mixture.
- Now, fold in the whipped egg whites.
- Fold in the strawberries.

- In another bowl, mix together the coffee and rum.
- Coat 1/2 of the ladyfingers in the coffee mixture slightly.
- In a serving bowl, arrange the remaining ladyfingers evenly and top with 1/2 of the mascarpone mixture, followed by the soaked ladyfingers and then remaining mascarpone mixture.
- Refrigerate, covered for at least 4 hours.
- Sift the cocoa powder over the tiramisu and serve with a garnishing of the strawberry halves.

Servings per Recipe: 8

Timing Information:

Preparation	15 mins
Total Time	4 hrs 15 mins

Nutritional Information:

Calories	171.7
Fat	7.6g
Cholesterol	105.6mg
Sodium	51.6mg
Carbohydrates	20.1g
Protein	4.1g

* Percent Daily Values are based on a 2,000 calorie diet.

Kid's Favorite Strawberries

Ingredients

- 18 strawberries
- 18 tsp Nutella

Directions

- Wash the strawberries and with the paper towels pat dry.
- Hull the strawberries and remove the center stem.
- Place about 1 tsp of the Nutella into each strawberry and serve.

Servings per Recipe: 6

Timing Information:

Preparation	10 mins
Total Time	10 mins

Nutritional Information:

Calories	111.6
Fat	5.6g
Cholesterol	0.0mg
Sodium	7.9mg
Carbohydrates	14.2g
Protein	1.2g

* Percent Daily Values are based on a 2,000 calorie diet.

Saturday Afternoon Drink

Ingredients

- 1 pint ripe fresh strawberries, washed & hulled
- 2 tbsp fresh lemon juice
- 2 tbsp fresh lime juice
- 1 tbsp sugar
- 1/4 C. club soda
- 1/2-1 C. ice cube

Directions

- Reserve 2 whole strawberries for the garnishing.
- In a blender, add the remaining strawberries and pulse till smooth.
- Add the remaining Ingredients and pulse till smooth and foamy.
- Transfer the mixture into 2 serving glasses and serve with a garnish of the strawberry.

Servings per Recipe: 2

Timing Information:

Preparation	5 mins
Total Time	6 mins

Nutritional Information:

Calories	88.8
Fat	0.5g
Cholesterol	0.0mg
Sodium	9.0mg
Carbohydrates	22.5g
Protein	1.3g

* Percent Daily Values are based on a 2,000 calorie diet.

Roman Strawberries

Ingredients

- 2 pints fresh strawberries

SAUCE

- 1 C. brown sugar
- 1/4 C. orange juice
- 2 C. sour cream

Directions

- In a bowl, add the brown sugar and juice and mix till smooth.
- Add the sour cream and mix till well combined.
- Divide the strawberries into serving bowls and serve with a topping with the cream sauce.

Servings per Recipe: 4

Timing Information:

Preparation	20 mins
Total Time	20 mins

Nutritional Information:

Calories	488.0
Fat	23.2g
Cholesterol	59.8mg
Sodium	109.1mg
Carbohydrates	70.9g
Protein	3.6g

* Percent Daily Values are based on a 2,000 calorie diet.

Fruit Salsa

Ingredients

- 2 1/2 C. finely chopped fresh strawberries
- 1 C. chopped green pepper
- 2 tbsp chopped green onions
- 2 tbsp minced fresh parsley
- 1/3 C. Catalina dressing
- 1 dash hot sauce
- Salt and pepper
- Tortilla chips

Directions

- In a bowl, mix together all the Ingredients except the tortilla chips.
- Refrigerate, covered for about 2 hours.
- Serve alongside the tortilla chips.

Servings per Recipe: 1

Timing Information:

Preparation	15 mins
Total Time	15 mins

Nutritional Information:

Calories	177.3
Fat	12.9g
Cholesterol	0.0mg
Sodium	237.2mg
Carbohydrates	16.3g
Protein	1.5g

* Percent Daily Values are based on a 2,000 calorie diet.

Cute Strawberry Desserts

Ingredients

- 1 (8 oz.) packages cream cheese, softened
- 1 (6 oz.) packages semi-sweet chocolate chips, melted
- 3/4 C. vanilla wafer crumbs
- 1/4 C. strawberry preserves
- 1/2 C. almonds, toasted finely chopped
- Powdered sugar

Directions

- In a bowl, add the cream cheese and with an electric mixer, beat on medium speed till fluffy.
- Add the melted chocolate and beat till smooth.
- Stir in the wafer crumbs and preserves and refrigerate, covered for at least 1 hour.
- Make 1-inch balls from the mixture and coat with the almonds.
- Transfer into airtight container and preserve in refrigerator.

Servings per Recipe: 1

Timing Information:

| Preparation | 15 mins |
| Total Time | 15 mins |

Nutritional Information:

Calories	761.3
Fat	49.9g
Cholesterol	62.3mg
Sodium	367.5mg
Carbohydrates	75.6g
Protein	11.7g

* Percent Daily Values are based on a 2,000 calorie diet.

Wednesday Breakfast Bread

Ingredients

- 1 C. sugar
- 1/2 C. butter, softened
- 2 eggs, separated
- 1/2 tsp almond extract
- 2 C. flour
- 1 tsp baking soda
- 1 tsp baking powder
- 1/2 tsp salt
- 1 1/2 C. fresh strawberries, sliced
- 3/4 C. slivered almonds

Directions

- Set your oven to 350 degrees F before doing anything else and grease a 9x5-inch loaf pan.
- In a bowl, add the sugar and butter and beat till creamy.
- Add the egg yolks and almond extract and beat till well combined.
- In another bowl, mix together the flour, baking soda, baking powder and salt.
- Add the flour mixture alternately with the strawberries into the butter mixture and mix till well combined.

- In a small bowl, add the egg whites and beat well.
- Fold the beaten egg whites and almonds into the flour mixture.
- Place the mixture into the prepared loaf pan evenly.
- Cook in the oven for about 45-50 minutes or till a toothpick inserted in the center comes out clean.

Servings per Recipe: 1

Timing Information:

| Preparation | 20 mins |
| Total Time | 1 hr 10 mins |

Nutritional Information:

Calories	3184.0
Fat	144.7g
Cholesterol	616.0mg
Sodium	3746.9mg
Carbohydrates	427.0g
Protein	57.9g

* Percent Daily Values are based on a 2,000 calorie diet.

Strawberry Melody

Ingredients

- 2 C. strawberries, cleaned and stemmed
- 1/3 C. white sugar
- 1 tsp vanilla

Directions

- Slice about 1/3 of the strawberries in half.
- In a pan, add the strawberries, sugar and vanilla on medium-high heat and cook for about 5 minutes, stirring occasionally.
- Remove from the heat and keep aside to cool slightly.
- In a blender, add about 1/2 of the sauce and pulse till smooth.
- Return the pureed sauce in the remaining and stir to combine.
- Transfer into airtight container and preserve in refrigerator.

Servings per Recipe: 4

Timing Information:

Preparation	20 mins
Total Time	20 mins

Nutritional Information:

Calories	90.5
Fat	0.2g
Cholesterol	0.0mg
Sodium	0.8mg
Carbohydrates	22.3g
Protein	0.4g

* Percent Daily Values are based on a 2,000 calorie diet.

Strawberry & Orange Spring Rolls with Strawberry Sauce

Ingredients

For Rolls:

- 4 1/2-oz. raw sugar
- 4 eggs
- 4 1/2-oz. unsalted butter
- Fresh juice and zest of 3 oranges
- Oil, as required
- 2 lbs fresh strawberries, hulled and chopped finely
- 8 spring roll sheets
- 2 tsps arrowroot powder
- 1 egg white

For Sauce:

- Chopped fresh strawberries, as required
- 3 3/4-oz. caster sugar
- 2 fluid oz. water
- 2 fluid oz. Grand Mariner

Directions

- For the rolls in a bowl, add raw sugar and eggs and beat till well combined and keep aside.
- In a pan, mix together butter, orange zest and orange juice and bring to a gentle simmer.
- Slowly, add the egg mixture, stirring continuously till the mixture becomes thick.
- Remove everything from the heat and let it cool completely.
- In a bowl, mix together the chopped strawberries and 1 1/2 tbsps of orange mixture.
- In a small bowl, mix together the arrowroot powder and egg white.
- Place the wrappers onto a smooth surface.
- Divide the strawberry mixture in the center of each wrapper evenly.
- Roll the wrappers around the filling and with your cornstarch mixture, brush the edges and press to seal completely.
- In a large cast-iron skillet or deep fryer, heat the oil.
- Carefully, add the rolls in the skillet in batches.
- Fry the rolls till golden brown and transfer onto paper towel lined plates to drain.
- Meanwhile for the sauce in a pan, mix together all the ingredients and simmer till strawberries become soft.
- Transfer the mixture into a blender and pulse till a puree forms.
- Serve the rolls with strawberry sauce.

Amount per serving: 4

Timing Information:

Preparation	30 mins
Total Time	45 mins

Nutritional Information:

Calories	733.2
Cholesterol	281.5mg
Sodium	183.7mg
Carbohydrates	105.6g
Protein	12.1g

* Percent Daily Values are based on a 2,000 calorie diet.

Strawberry & Banana Spring Rolls

Ingredients

- 12 large square rice paper sheets
- 8 medium strawberries, hulled and sliced
- 2 bananas, peeled and sliced
- 7-oz. strawberry flavored vegan soy yogurt
- Fresh mint leaves, for garnishing

Directions

- Soak the rice papers, one by one in a bowl of warm water till soft and transfer onto paper towels.
- Place the rice papers onto a smooth surface.
- Divide the strawberry and banana slices in the center of each rice paper evenly.
- Fold the inner sides of wrappers around the filling and roll tightly.
- Cut each roll in half and serve with yogurt and a garnishing of mint.

Amount per serving: 4

Timing Information:

Preparation	10 mins
Total Time	20 mins

Nutritional Information:

Calories	60.1
Cholesterol	0.0mg
Sodium	0.8mg
Carbohydrates	15.3g
Protein	0.8g

* Percent Daily Values are based on a 2,000 calorie diet.

Strawberry Pineapple Gazpacho

Ingredients

- 1/2 C. diced pineapple
- 1/2 C. diced strawberry
- 1 C. sliced grapes
- 3/4 C. blueberries
- 1 C. apple juice
- 1/2 C. orange juice
- 1/4 tsp black pepper
- 1/2 orange, segmented

Directions

- Get a bowl, combine: blueberries, pineapple, grapes, and strawberries.
- Stir the mix then place a covering of plastic on the bowl.
- Put everything in the fridge until chilled, then divide the mix between serving bowls.
- Top each serving with the orange and pepper.
- Enjoy.

Amount per serving: 4

Timing Information:

Preparation	20 mins
Total Time	25 mins

Nutritional Information:

Calories	109.2
Fat	0.3g
Cholesterol	0.0mg
Sodium	3.6mg
Carbohydrates	27.4g
Protein	1.1g

* Percent Daily Values are based on a 2,000 calorie diet.

Chocolaty Strawberry Filled Crepes

Ingredients

CREPES

- 1 egg, beaten
- 1/4 C. skim milk
- 1/3 C. water
- 1 tbsp vegetable oil
- 2/3 C. all-purpose flour
- 1/4 tsp white sugar
- 1 pinch salt

FILLING

- 1/2 C. semisweet chocolate chips
- 1 C. sliced fresh strawberries
- 3/4 C. frozen whipped topping, thawed

Directions

- For the crepes in a large bowl, add the milk, oil, egg and water and beat till well combined.
- Add the remaining ingredients and beat till smooth.
- Lightly, grease a griddle and heat on medium-high heat.

- Place about 1/4 C. of the mixture and tilt the pan to spread it evenly.
- Cook for about 2-5 minutes, flipping once.
- Repeat with the remaining mixture.
- For the filling, in a pan, add the chocolate chips on low heat and cook, stirring continuously till melted completely and remove from heat.
- Divide the melted chocolate in the center of the crepes, followed by strawberries and roll around the filling.
- Place the whipped topping over the crepes and serve.

Amount per serving (4 total)

Timing Information:

Preparation	5 m
Cooking	15 m
Total Time	10 m

Nutritional Information:

Calories	279 kcal
Fat	13.4 g
Carbohydrates	36.3g
Protein	5.4 g
Cholesterol	47 mg
Sodium	27 mg

* Percent Daily Values are based on a 2,000 calorie diet.

A Strawberry Shortcake Sweet Doughnut

Ingredients:
- 2 cups heavy whipping cream
- 1/2 cup confectioners' sugar
- 1 tsp vanilla extract
- 4 glazed doughnuts, halved horizontally
- 1 quart strawberries, hulled and sliced

Directions
- Get a bowl, mix: vanilla extract, cream, and sugar.
- Use electric mixer to form whipped cream.
- Take one doughnut and cut it in half. Top with ¼ cup of cream.
- Top cream with ¼ cup of strawberries.
- Top with remaining doughnut half. Continue for remaining doughnuts.
- Enjoy.

Serving Size: 4 servings

Timing Information:

Preparation	Cooking	Total Time
15 mins		15 mins

Nutritional Information:

Calories	766 kcal
Carbohydrates	57.4 g
Cholesterol	167 mg
Fat	58.2 g
Fiber	3.8 g
Protein	7.3 g
Sodium	252 mg

* Percent Daily Values are based on a 2,000 calorie diet.

Jelly Doughnut II

Ingredients:
- 3 eggs, beaten
- 1/2 cup milk
- 1/2 tsp vanilla extract
- 1/4 cup sugar
- 1 cup all-purpose flour
- 1/2 tsp baking powder
- 1/4 tsp salt
- canola oil
- 10 slices white bread
- strawberry (or any flavor) jam
- confectioners' sugar

Directions
- Get a bowl, mix: sugar, eggs, vanilla, and milk.
- Grab a 2nd bowl, mix: salt, flour, and baking powder.
- Mix both bowls.
- Get a deep fryer. Set oil to 375 degrees.
- Trim the crusts off of white bread slices. Use to make jam sandwiches.
- Cut each sandwich in half coat with egg mixture, by dipping.
- Fry each sandwich for 4 mins, until golden. Set aside to remove excess oils.

- Cover everything with confectioner's sugar.

Serving Size: 40 doughnuts

Timing Information:

Preparation	Cooking	Total Time
20 mins	20 mins	40 mins

Nutritional Information:

Calories	263 kcal
Carbohydrates	13.4 g
Cholesterol	14 mg
Fat	23.1 g
Fiber	0.3 g
Protein	1.4 g
Sodium	70 mg

* Percent Daily Values are based on a 2,000 calorie diet.

THANKS FOR READING! JOIN THE CLUB AND KEEP ON COOKING WITH 6 MORE COOKBOOKS....

http://bit.ly/1TdrStv

 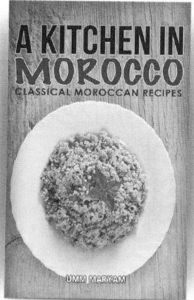 

To grab the box sets simply follow the link mentioned above, or tap one of book covers.

This will take you to a page where you can simply enter your email address and a PDF version of the box sets will be emailed to you.

Hope you are ready for some serious cooking!

http://bit.ly/1TdrStv

Come On...
Let's Be Friends :)

We adore our readers and love connecting with them socially.

Like BookSumo on Facebook and let's get social!

Facebook

And also check out the BookSumo Cooking Blog.

Food Lover Blog

Made in the USA
San Bernardino, CA
17 May 2019